UNLEASH CULINARY MAGIC WITH THE 30-MINUTE ANDALUSIAN COOKBOOK

A Gastronomic Symphony of Over 50 Irresistible Recipes

McArthur Light

30-Minute Andalusian Cookbook

Copyright © 2024 McArthur Light

INTRODUCTION

Welcome to the culinary journey of "30-Minute Andalusian Cookbook: A Gastronomic Symphony with Over 100 Irresistible Recipes." In this delectable adventure, we invite you to discover the vibrant flavors and rich traditions of Andalusian cuisine, masterfully curated for those seeking both speed and culinary excellence.

Our cookbook is a celebration of the quick and tantalizing, offering a diverse collection of recipes that go from kitchen to table in just 30 minutes. Whether you're a seasoned chef or a novice in the kitchen, these dishes are crafted to elevate your cooking experience without compromising on taste.

From sizzling tapas to luscious desserts, each chapter unfolds a new chapter in the art of creating mouthwatering masterpieces with minimal time investment. Join us on this culinary odyssey as we embrace the essence of Andalusia's culinary heritage and transform your everyday meals into extraordinary moments.

Dive into the pages ahead, where simplicity meets sophistication, and the joy of cooking is as swift as it is savory. Let the aromas of Andalusian spices and the ease of our recipes inspire you to embark on a delightful journey of flavors, bringing the essence of Southern Spain to your home kitchen.

CHAPTER 1: SIZZLING STARTERS

1.1 Quick Patatas Bravas

Ingredients:
- 4 large potatoes, diced
- 1/4 cup olive oil
- 2 teaspoons smoked paprika
- 1 teaspoon garlic powder
- Salt and pepper to taste
- 1/2 cup tomato sauce
- 1 tablespoon spicy chili sauce
- 2 tablespoons chopped fresh parsley

Steps:
1. Preheat the oven to 425°F (220°C).
2. Toss the diced potatoes with olive oil, smoked paprika, garlic powder, salt, and pepper.
3. Spread the seasoned potatoes on a baking sheet in a single layer.
4. Roast in the preheated oven for 20-25 minutes or until golden and crispy.
5. While the potatoes are roasting, combine tomato sauce and spicy chili sauce in a small saucepan. Simmer on low heat for 5 minutes.

6. Once the potatoes are done, transfer them to a serving platter.

7. Drizzle the spicy tomato sauce over the roasted potatoes.

8. Garnish with chopped fresh parsley.

9. Serve hot and enjoy this tantalizing tapas delight!

Total Time: 30 minutes

CHAPTER 2: ZESTY LEMON GARLIC SHRIMP

Ingredients:
- 1 pound large shrimp, peeled and deveined
- 4 cloves garlic, minced
- 1/4 cup fresh lemon juice
- 2 tablespoons olive oil
- 1 teaspoon paprika
- 1/2 teaspoon red pepper flakes (adjust to taste)
- Salt and black pepper to taste
- 2 tablespoons fresh parsley, chopped (for garnish)

Cooking Time: 20 minutes

Servings: 4

Steps:

1. Marinate the Shrimp:
   - In a bowl, combine the shrimp, minced garlic, lemon juice, olive oil, paprika, red pepper flakes, salt, and black pepper.

- Toss the shrimp until well-coated and let it marinate for 10 minutes to allow the flavors to meld.

2. Preheat the Skillet:

- Heat a large skillet over medium-high heat. Add a splash of olive oil to coat the bottom of the skillet.

3. Cook the Shrimp:

- Transfer the marinated shrimp to the hot skillet in a single layer. Cook for 2-3 minutes on each side or until the shrimp turn pink and opaque.

4. Add Freshness:

- Squeeze additional fresh lemon juice over the shrimp while cooking for an extra burst of citrus flavor.

5. Garnish and Serve:

- Sprinkle chopped fresh parsley over the cooked shrimp for a burst of color and freshness.

6. Serve Hot:

- Remove the skillet from heat and serve the zesty lemon garlic shrimp immediately.

Pro Tips:
- Serve over a bed of cooked couscous or with crusty bread to soak up the flavorful juices.
- Experiment with adding a splash of white wine to the marinade for an extra layer of depth.
- Don't overcook the shrimp to keep them tender and juicy.

Enjoy this quick and flavorful Zesty Lemon Garlic Shrimp that captures the essence of Andalusian cuisine in just 20 minutes!

CHAPTER 3: PAELLA PERFECTION

SEAFOOD PAELLA

Ingredients:
- 2 cups bomba rice
- 1 lb mixed seafood (shrimp, mussels, squid)
- 1 onion, finely chopped
- 3 cloves garlic, minced
- 1 red bell pepper, diced
- 1 tomato, grated
- 1/2 cup frozen peas
- 4 cups seafood or vegetable broth
- 1 teaspoon saffron threads
- 1 teaspoon smoked paprika
- Salt and pepper to taste
- 1/4 cup olive oil
- Lemon wedges for serving

Cooking Time: 30 minutes

Steps:

1. **Prepare the Broth:**

   - Heat the seafood or vegetable broth in a saucepan. Add saffron threads and let them steep.

2. Sauté Aromatics:
   - In a large paella pan, heat olive oil over medium heat. Sauté onions and garlic until translucent.

3. Add Rice and Paprika:
   - Stir in bomba rice and smoked paprika, coating the rice evenly with the oil and spices.

4. Incorporate Vegetables:
   - Add diced red bell pepper and grated tomato. Cook until the vegetables soften.

5. Pour in Broth:
   - Pour in the saffron-infused broth. Season with salt and pepper. Allow the mixture to simmer for 10 minutes.

6. Arrange Seafood:
   - Nestle the mixed seafood into the rice mixture. Distribute evenly.

7. Scatter Peas:
   - Sprinkle frozen peas over the top. Cover the pan and let it simmer for an additional 10-15

minutes or until the rice is cooked and the seafood is done.

8. Check for Doneness:
   - Ensure the rice has absorbed the liquid and has a slightly crispy bottom known as "socarrat."

9. Serve:
   - Garnish with lemon wedges. Serve the paella directly from the pan for an authentic touch.

Enjoy the rich flavors of this Seafood Paella, a dish that captures the essence of Andalusian cuisine in just 30 minutes!

CHAPTER 4: FLAVORSOME FISH DISHES

Recipe 1: Lemon Herb Baked Cod

Ingredients:
- 4 cod fillets
- 2 tablespoons olive oil
- 2 cloves garlic, minced
- 1 lemon (zested and juiced)
- 1 teaspoon dried thyme
- Salt and pepper to taste
- Fresh parsley for garnish

Steps:
1. Preheat the oven to 400°F (200°C).
2. Place cod fillets on a baking sheet lined with parchment paper.
3. In a small bowl, mix olive oil, minced garlic, lemon zest, lemon juice, dried thyme, salt, and pepper.
4. Brush the cod fillets with the lemon herb mixture, ensuring they are evenly coated.
5. Bake in the preheated oven for 15-18 minutes or until the cod flakes easily with a fork.

6. Garnish with fresh parsley before serving.

Cooking Time: 15-18 minutes

Pro Tip for Readers:
Time may vary based on your oven and the thickness of the cod fillets. Keep an eye on the fish to prevent overcooking. Enjoy this dish with a side of Mediterranean quinoa for a complete and delightful meal!

RECIPE 2: ANDALUSIAN-STYLE GRILLED SARDINES

Ingredients:
- 8 fresh sardines, gutted and cleaned
- 3 tablespoons olive oil
- 2 cloves garlic, minced
- 1 teaspoon smoked paprika
- Salt and pepper to taste
- Lemon wedges for serving

Steps:
1. Preheat the grill to medium-high heat.
2. In a bowl, mix olive oil, minced garlic, smoked paprika, salt, and pepper.

3. Brush the sardines with the olive oil mixture, ensuring they are well-coated.

4. Grill the sardines for 3-4 minutes per side or until they are cooked through and have a nice char.

5. Serve with lemon wedges.

Cooking Time: 6-8 minutes

Pro Tip for Readers:

Grilling time may vary based on the size of the sardines and the heat of your grill. Be attentive and savor the authentic Andalusian flavors with this simple yet delightful dish!

Chapter 5: Mouthwatering Main Courses - Garlic Rosemary Lamb Chops

---

Ingredients:
- 8 lamb chops
- 4 cloves garlic, minced
- 2 tablespoons fresh rosemary, chopped
- 3 tablespoons olive oil
- Salt and pepper to taste

Steps:
1. Preheat your oven to 400°F (200°C).
2. In a small bowl, mix minced garlic, chopped rosemary, olive oil, salt, and pepper to create a flavorful marinade.
3. Pat the lamb chops dry with paper towels and generously coat them with the marinade.
4. Allow the lamb chops to marinate for at least 15 minutes to absorb the flavors.
5. Heat a skillet over medium-high heat and sear the lamb chops for 2-3 minutes on each side, or until browned.
6. Transfer the seared lamb chops to a baking dish and roast in the preheated oven for

approximately 12–15 minutes for medium-rare, or adjust to your desired doneness.

7. Remove from the oven and let the lamb chops rest for 5 minutes before serving.

Cooking Time:
- Marinating: 15 minutes
- Searing: 6–8 minutes
- Roasting: 12–15 minutes
- Resting: 5 minutes

Pro Tip: Cooking times may vary based on the thickness of the lamb chops and your preferred level of doneness. Always use a meat thermometer to ensure the lamb reaches your desired internal temperature.

CHAPTER 6: VIBRANT VEGETARIAN DELIGHTS

6.1 Chickpea and Spinach Stew

Ingredients:
- 2 cans (15 oz each) chickpeas, drained and rinsed
- 1 onion, finely chopped
- 3 cloves garlic, minced
- 1 can (14 oz) diced tomatoes
- 1 bunch fresh spinach, washed and chopped
- 1 teaspoon ground cumin
- 1 teaspoon smoked paprika
- 1/2 teaspoon cayenne pepper
- 2 tablespoons olive oil
- Salt and pepper to taste
- Fresh parsley for garnish

Cooking Time: 30 minutes

Steps:
1. Heat olive oil in a large pot over medium heat. Add chopped onions and cook until softened.

2. Stir in minced garlic, ground cumin, smoked paprika, and cayenne pepper. Cook for an additional 2 minutes until fragrant.

3. Pour in the diced tomatoes with their juices. Allow the mixture to simmer for 10 minutes, stirring occasionally.

4. Add the drained chickpeas to the pot and cook for an additional 10 minutes, allowing the flavors to meld.

5. Toss in the chopped spinach and cook until wilted. Season with salt and pepper to taste.

6. Serve the stew hot, garnished with fresh parsley.

Cooking Tip: Feel free to customize the spice levels according to your taste preferences. Add a squeeze of lemon juice for an extra burst of freshness.

Pro Tip: Cooking times may vary depending on your stove and altitude. Keep an eye on the simmering times to achieve the perfect texture for your chickpea and spinach stew. Enjoy the process!

CHAPTER 7: ENCHANTING DESSERTS - CHURROS WITH CHOCOLATE DIPPING SAUCE

Ingredients:
- 1 cup water
- 2 1/2 tablespoons white sugar
- 1/2 teaspoon salt
- 2 tablespoons vegetable oil
- 1 cup all-purpose flour
- 2 cups vegetable oil (for frying)

For Coating:
- 1/4 cup white sugar
- 1/2 teaspoon ground cinnamon

For Chocolate Dipping Sauce:
- 1/2 cup dark chocolate, finely chopped
- 1/2 cup heavy cream
- 1 tablespoon unsalted butter

Steps:

1. In a saucepan, combine water, sugar, salt, and 2 tablespoons of vegetable oil. Bring to a boil over medium heat.

2. Remove the saucepan from heat and stir in the flour until the mixture forms a ball. Let it cool for a couple of minutes.

3. Heat 2 cups of vegetable oil in a deep fryer or large, heavy pan to 375°F (190°C).

4. Spoon the dough into a piping bag fitted with a star tip. Pipe 6-inch strips of dough directly into the hot oil, cutting with scissors. Fry until golden brown, turning once. This should take about 2-3 minutes per side.

5. Remove the churros from the oil and drain on paper towels. While still warm, toss them in a mixture of sugar and cinnamon until evenly coated.

Chocolate Dipping Sauce:

6. In a small saucepan, heat the heavy cream until it just begins to boil.

7. Pour the hot cream over the finely chopped dark chocolate in a heatproof bowl. Let it sit for a minute, then stir until smooth.

8. Add the unsalted butter to the chocolate mixture, stirring until fully incorporated.

9. Serve the warm churros with the rich chocolate dipping sauce.

Cooking Time:
- Churros: Approximately 15-20 minutes
- Chocolate Dipping Sauce: 5 minutes

Pro Tip:
Watch the oil temperature closely while frying the churros to ensure they achieve that perfect golden crispiness. Cooking times may vary based on the size of your churros and the specific heat of your oil. Adjust accordingly for the best results!

CHAPTER 8: REFRESHING BEVERAGES

Sparkling Ginger Lemonade

Ingredients:
- 1 cup fresh lemon juice
- 1/2 cup ginger syrup
- 1/2 cup simple syrup
- 2 cups sparkling water
- Ice cubes
- Lemon slices and mint for garnish

Steps:
1. **Prepare Ginger Syrup:** In a saucepan, combine 1 cup of water, 1 cup of sugar, and a 1-inch piece of fresh ginger (peeled and sliced). Simmer for 10 minutes, then strain and cool.

2. **Make Simple Syrup:** Mix 1 cup of water and 1 cup of sugar in a small saucepan. Heat until the sugar dissolves, then let it cool.

3. **Squeeze Fresh Lemon Juice:**Juice enough lemons to yield 1 cup of fresh lemon juice.

4. **Combine Ingredients:** In a pitcher, mix the fresh lemon juice, ginger syrup, and simple syrup. Stir well.

5. **Add Sparkling Water:** Pour in the sparkling water and stir gently to combine.

6. **Chill and Serve:** Refrigerate the lemonade for at least 30 minutes. Serve over ice and garnish with lemon slices and fresh mint.

Cooking Time: 10 minutes (plus 30 minutes chilling time)

Pro Tip: Enjoy this refreshing beverage on a warm day or as a delightful accompaniment to your favorite dishes. Keep in mind that chilling time may vary, so feel free to adjust it to your preference.

CHAPTER 9: SAVORY SIDES - GARLIC HERB AIOLI

Ingredients:
- 1 cup mayonnaise
- 3 cloves garlic, minced
- 1 tablespoon Dijon mustard
- 1 tablespoon fresh lemon juice
- 1 teaspoon fresh parsley, finely chopped
- 1 teaspoon fresh chives, finely chopped
- Salt and pepper to taste

Steps:
1. In a medium bowl, combine mayonnaise, minced garlic, Dijon mustard, and fresh lemon juice.
2. Mix well until all ingredients are thoroughly incorporated.
3. Add the finely chopped parsley and chives to the mixture.
4. Season the aioli with salt and pepper according to your taste preferences.
5. Whisk the ingredients together until the herbs are evenly distributed throughout the aioli.

6. Cover the bowl and refrigerate for at least 30 minutes to allow the flavors to meld.

Cooking Time:30 minutes (including refrigeration time)

Pro Tip for Readers:
Watch the clock as you let the aioli chill – the longer it sits, the more robust the flavors become. Feel free to adjust the garlic and herbs to suit your taste. This versatile aioli is a perfect companion for fries, sandwiches, or as a dipping sauce for veggies. Enjoy the creamy goodness, and remember, patience is the key to culinary perfection!

CHAPTER 10: DELECTABLE DESSERT TAPAS

Ingredients:
- 1 cup all-purpose flour
  1 cup water
- 1/4 cup unsalted butter
- 2 tablespoons sugar
- 1/4 teaspoon salt
- 2 large eggs
- Vegetable oil for frying
- 1/2 cup sugar (for coating)
- 1 teaspoon ground cinnamon (for coating)

Steps:

1. In a saucepan, combine water, butter, sugar, and salt. Bring to a boil over medium heat.
2. Remove from heat and add the flour all at once, stirring vigorously until the mixture forms a ball.

3. Allow the mixture to cool for a couple of minutes, then beat in the eggs one at a time until smooth.

4. Heat vegetable oil in a deep pan to 375°F (190°C).

5. Spoon the churro batter into a piping bag fitted with a star tip.

6. Pipe 3-inch strips of dough into the hot oil, using scissors to cut the dough.

7. Fry until golden brown, about 2-3 minutes per side. Remove with a slotted spoon and drain on paper towels.

8. In a bowl, combine sugar and ground cinnamon. Roll the warm churros in the mixture to coat evenly.

Cooking Time:
- Preparation: 15 minutes
- Cooking: 15 minutes
- Total Time: 30 minutes

Pro Tip:
Each batch of churros may have a slightly different cooking time, depending on factors like oil temperature and thickness of the dough. Keep an eye on the color – a golden brown hue indicates a perfect, crispy churro. Enjoy these treats immediately for the best experience, and

don't forget to share the joy with friends and family!

CHAPTER 11: QUICK AND EASY BREAKFASTS

Breakfast Burritos with Chorizo and Eggs

Ingredients:
- 1 tablespoon olive oil
- 1/2 cup diced chorizo
- 4 large eggs, beaten
- Salt and pepper to taste
- 1 cup shredded cheddar cheese
- 4 large flour tortillas
- 1 avocado, sliced
- Salsa and sour cream for serving

Cooking Time: 20 minutes

Steps:
1. Heat olive oil in a skillet over medium heat.
2. Add diced chorizo and cook until browned and slightly crispy, about 5 minutes.
3. Push chorizo to the side of the pan and pour beaten eggs into the empty side.
4. Season eggs with salt and pepper and scramble until just cooked through, about 3-4 minutes.

5. Sprinkle shredded cheddar cheese over the eggs and chorizo, allowing it to melt.

6. Warm tortillas in a separate pan or microwave for 20 seconds.

7. Assemble burritos by placing a portion of the egg and chorizo mixture onto each tortilla.

8. Top with sliced avocado and fold the sides of the tortilla over the filling.

9. Serve with salsa and sour cream on the side.

Pro Tip for Readers:

Feel free to customize your breakfast burrito with additional ingredients like diced tomatoes, onions, or cilantro. Cooking times may vary based on stove heat and personal preferences, so keep an eye on the eggs for the perfect consistency. Enjoy the flexibility of this recipe and experiment with your favorite flavors!

CHAPTER 12: SAUCY CREATIONS - GARLIC LEMON AIOLI

Ingredients:
- 1 cup mayonnaise
- 2 cloves garlic, minced
- 1 tablespoon fresh lemon juice
- 1 teaspoon Dijon mustard
- Salt and pepper to taste
- 2 tablespoons fresh parsley, finely chopped (optional for garnish)

Cooking Time: 10 minutes

Servings: Approximately 1 cup

Steps:

1. In a small mixing bowl, combine mayonnaise, minced garlic, fresh lemon juice, and Dijon mustard.

2. Whisk the ingredients together until well combined, ensuring the garlic is evenly distributed.

3. Season the aioli with salt and pepper to taste. Adjust the seasoning according to your preference.

4. For added freshness, fold in finely chopped fresh parsley into the aioli. This step is optional but highly recommended for a burst of flavor.

5. Cover the bowl and refrigerate the garlic lemon aioli for at least 30 minutes before serving. This allows the flavors to meld and intensify.

6. Once chilled, give the aioli a final stir and taste. Adjust the seasoning if necessary.

7. Garnish with additional chopped parsley if desired.

Pro Tip for Readers:
Cooking times may vary based on the temperature of your ingredients and personal preferences. Feel free to experiment with the garlic lemon aioli, adjusting the garlic, lemon, or other seasonings to suit your taste. Enjoy the creative process and make this recipe your own!

CHAPTER 13: RAVISHING RICE DISHES

Dish: Speedy Saffron Rice Pilaf

Ingredients:
- 1 cup basmati rice
- 2 cups vegetable broth
- 1/2 teaspoon saffron threads
- 2 tablespoons olive oil
- 1 small onion, finely chopped
- 2 cloves garlic, minced
- 1/4 cup slivered almonds
- Salt and pepper to taste
- Fresh parsley for garnish

Cooking Time:
- Preparation: 10 minutes
- Cooking: 20 minutes
- Total: 30 minutes

Instructions:
1. Rinse the basmati rice under cold water until the water runs clear. Set aside.

2. In a small bowl, steep the saffron threads in 1/4 cup of warm vegetable broth. Let it sit for 5 minutes.

3. In a medium-sized saucepan, heat olive oil over medium heat. Add chopped onions and garlic, sauté until golden brown.

4. Add the rinsed rice to the pan and stir for 2-3 minutes until the rice is lightly toasted.

5. Pour in the saffron-infused vegetable broth and remaining broth. Season with salt and pepper to taste.

6. Bring the mixture to a boil, then reduce the heat to low, cover, and simmer for 15 minutes or until the rice is tender and the liquid is absorbed.

7. In a separate pan, toast slivered almonds until golden brown.

8. Once the rice is cooked, fluff it with a fork and gently fold in the toasted almonds.

9. Garnish with fresh parsley and serve hot.

Pro Tip:
Watch the rice closely during the last 5 minutes of cooking. Cooking times may vary based on your stove and pan, ensuring the perfect fluffy texture for your pilaf. Adjust heat accordingly to avoid overcooking. Enjoy this aromatic dish as a flavorful side or pair it with your favorite main course.

CHAPTER 12: SAUCY CREATIONS

Romesco Sauce for Dipping

Ingredients:
- 2 red bell peppers, roasted and peeled
- 1 cup almonds, toasted
- 3 cloves garlic, minced
- 1/4 cup tomato paste
- 1/3 cup red wine vinegar
- 1 teaspoon smoked paprika
- 1/2 teaspoon cayenne pepper
- Salt and pepper to taste
- 1/2 cup extra-virgin olive oil

Cooking Time: 20 minutes

Steps:
1. In a food processor, combine roasted red peppers, toasted almonds, minced garlic, tomato paste, red wine vinegar, smoked paprika, cayenne pepper, salt, and pepper.
2. Pulse until the mixture is finely chopped.

3. With the food processor running, slowly drizzle in the olive oil until the sauce reaches a smooth consistency.

4. Taste and adjust seasoning if necessary.

5. Transfer the Romesco sauce to a bowl and refrigerate for at least 30 minutes to allow the flavors to meld.

Pro Tip:

Cooking times may vary based on your equipment and preferences. Feel free to adjust the spice level or experiment with different types of nuts for a unique twist.

CHAPTER 13: RAVISHING RICE DISHES

Recipe: Tomato Basil Arroz con Pollo

Ingredients:
- 1 1/2 cups long-grain rice
- 4 boneless, skinless chicken thighs
- 1 large onion, finely chopped
- 2 bell peppers (any color), diced
- 3 cloves garlic, minced
- 1 can (14 oz) diced tomatoes
- 2 cups chicken broth
- 1 teaspoon smoked paprika
- 1 teaspoon ground cumin
- Salt and pepper to taste
- Fresh basil leaves for garnish

Cooking Time:
- Preparation: 10 minutes
- Cooking: 25 minutes
- Total Time: 35 minutes

Steps:
1. Rinse the rice under cold water until the water runs clear. Set aside.

2. In a large skillet or paella pan, brown the chicken thighs over medium-high heat for about 3 minutes per side. Remove and set aside.

3. In the same pan, sauté the chopped onion until translucent, then add diced bell peppers and minced garlic. Cook for an additional 2-3 minutes until the vegetables are softened.

4. Stir in the rice and cook for 2 minutes, allowing the grains to toast slightly.

5. Pour in the diced tomatoes, chicken broth, smoked paprika, ground cumin, salt, and pepper. Mix well.

6. Nestle the browned chicken thighs into the rice mixture.

7. Bring the mixture to a boil, then reduce the heat to low. Cover and simmer for 20-25 minutes or until the rice is tender and the chicken is cooked through.

8. Garnish with fresh basil leaves before serving.

Pro Tip:
As cooking times can vary, especially with different stovetops or rice varieties, it's advisable to periodically check the rice's texture. Adjust the heat if needed and use a fork to fluff the rice to ensure it's perfectly cooked. Enjoy the savory aroma as it fills your kitchen, and savor the

delightful flavors of this Tomato Basil Arroz con Pollo!

CHAPTER 14: CITRUS-INFUSED DELIGHTS

---

1. Orange Almond Cake

**Ingredients:
- 2 cups all-purpose flour
- 1 cup almond meal
- 1 1/2 cups sugar
- 1 cup unsalted butter, softened
- 4 large eggs
- 1 cup fresh orange juice
- Zest of 2 oranges
- 1 teaspoon baking powder
- 1/2 teaspoon baking soda
- 1/2 teaspoon salt
- Powdered sugar for dusting (optional)

Steps:
1. Preheat your oven to 350°F (175°C) and grease a round cake pan.
2. In a bowl, whisk together the flour, almond meal, baking powder, baking soda, and salt. Set aside.

3. In another bowl, cream together the softened butter and sugar until light and fluffy.
4. Add the eggs one at a time, beating well after each addition.
5. Gradually add the dry ingredients to the wet ingredients, alternating with the orange juice. Mix until just combined.
6. Stir in the orange zest, ensuring it is evenly distributed throughout the batter.
7. Pour the batter into the prepared cake pan and smooth the top.
8. Bake for 40-45 minutes or until a toothpick inserted into the center comes out clean.
9. Allow the cake to cool in the pan for 10 minutes, then transfer it to a wire rack to cool completely.
10. Dust with powdered sugar before serving if desired.

Cooking Time:40-45 minutes

Pro Prompt:
As ovens may vary, keep an eye on your orange almond cake as it bakes. The delightful aroma will guide you, and a toothpick inserted into the center should come out clean when it's perfectly done. Enjoy the citrus-infused bliss of this delectable treat!

Chapter 15: Effortless Empanadas

Ingredients:
- 2 cups cooked shredded chicken
- 1 cup diced bell peppers (assorted colors)
- 1/2 cup chopped onion
- 1/2 cup black beans, drained and rinsed
- 1 cup shredded Monterey Jack cheese
- 1 teaspoon ground cumin
- 1 teaspoon smoked paprika
- Salt and pepper to taste
- 2 packages refrigerated pie crusts (4 crusts total)
- Egg wash (1 beaten egg with a splash of water)

Cooking Time:
- Preparation: 15 minutes
- Cooking: 15 minutes
- Total Time: 30 minutes

Cooking Steps:

1. Preheat the Oven:
  - Preheat your oven to 375°F (190°C).

2. Sauté the Vegetables:
   - In a skillet over medium heat, sauté the chopped onion and diced bell peppers until they are softened and slightly caramelized.

3. Prepare the Filling:
   - In a large mixing bowl, combine the shredded chicken, sautéed vegetables, black beans, shredded cheese, cumin, smoked paprika, salt, and pepper. Mix until well combined.

4. Roll Out the Dough:
   - Roll out the refrigerated pie crusts on a floured surface. Using a round cutter or a glass, cut out circles approximately 4-5 inches in diameter.

5. Fill and Seal:
   - Place a spoonful of the chicken mixture in the center of each dough circle. Fold the dough in half, creating a half-moon shape, and press the edges to seal. You can use a fork to crimp the edges for a decorative touch.

6. Brush with Egg Wash:
   - Brush the empanadas with the egg wash. This will give them a beautiful golden color when baked.

7. Bake to Perfection:

- Arrange the empanadas on a baking sheet lined with parchment paper. Bake in the preheated oven for about 15 minutes or until they are golden brown and crispy.

8. Serve and Enjoy:

- Allow the empanadas to cool for a few minutes before serving. They can be enjoyed on their own or with your favorite dipping sauce.

Pro Tip for Readers:

Cooking times may vary depending on your oven, so keep an eye on the empanadas for that perfect golden finish. Enjoy the delightful aroma as they bake, and adjust the cooking time accordingly for your desired level of crispiness.

CHAPTER 16: SPANISH STREET FOOD

Ingredients:
- 1 lb small potatoes, diced
- 1 cup spicy tomato sauce
- 1/2 cup mayonnaise
- 2 tsp smoked paprika
- 1 lb firm white fish fillets, cut into strips
- 8 small flour tortillas
- 1 cup shredded lettuce
- 1 cup diced tomatoes
- 1/2 cup chopped fresh cilantro
- Lime wedges for serving

Steps:

1. Prepare the Potatoes:
  - Boil the diced potatoes until tender, about 10 minutes.
  - Drain and set aside.

2. Create the Sauce Duo:
  - Mix the spicy tomato sauce with 1 teaspoon of smoked paprika.

- In a separate bowl, combine mayonnaise with the remaining smoked paprika.

3. Cook the Fish Strips:
- Season the fish strips with salt and pepper.
- Heat a pan over medium-high heat and cook the fish for 2-3 minutes per side until golden and cooked through.

4. Assemble the Tacos:
- Warm the flour tortillas.
- Spread a spoonful of the tomato sauce on each tortilla.
- Place a handful of shredded lettuce on top, followed by the diced tomatoes.

5. Add the Potatoes and Fish:
- Distribute the boiled potatoes and cooked fish strips evenly among the tortillas.

6. Drizzle with Sauces:
- Generously drizzle the smoked paprika mayo over the tacos.
- Finish by adding a dollop of the spicy tomato sauce.

7. Garnish and Serve:
- Sprinkle fresh cilantro over the top.

- Serve with lime wedges on the side.

Estimated Cooking Time: 25 minutes

Pro Tip: Customize your tacos with additional toppings like sliced avocado, pickled jalapeños, or a squeeze of extra lime juice. The joy of street food lies in making it your own!

47

CHAPTER 17: CRISPY BITES

Piquillo Pepper Poppers

Ingredients:
- 12 Piquillo peppers, drained
- 1 cup cream cheese, softened
- 1/2 cup Manchego cheese, grated
- 1/4 cup fresh parsley, chopped
- 1 clove garlic, minced
- Salt and pepper to taste
- 1 cup breadcrumbs
- 2 eggs, beaten
- Vegetable oil for frying

Steps:
1. In a mixing bowl, combine cream cheese, Manchego cheese, parsley, garlic, salt, and pepper. Mix until well blended.
2. Carefully stuff each Piquillo pepper with the cheese mixture, ensuring they are fully filled.
3. In one bowl, place breadcrumbs. In another, place beaten eggs.

4. Dip each stuffed pepper into the beaten eggs, ensuring even coating, then roll in breadcrumbs until fully coated.

5. Heat vegetable oil in a deep pan to 350°F (180°C).

6. Fry the stuffed peppers until golden brown, approximately 3 minutes per side.

7. Remove and drain on a paper towel.

8. Serve immediately and enjoy the crispy, cheesy goodness!

Cooking Time: Approximately 20 minutes

Pro Prompt:
As cooking times may vary, keep an eye on the temperature of your oil and adjust frying time accordingly for that perfect crispy texture. Don't forget to share your twist on these poppers – creativity in the kitchen is always encouraged!

CHAPTER 18: SUN-KISSED SALADS

Ingredients:
- 2 cups cherry tomatoes, halved
- 1 cup cucumber, diced
- 1 cup red onion, thinly sliced
- 1 cup feta cheese, crumbled
- 1/2 cup Kalamata olives, pitted and halved
- 1/4 cup fresh basil, chopped
- 2 tablespoons extra virgin olive oil
- 1 tablespoon red wine vinegar
- Salt and pepper to taste

Steps:
1. In a large salad bowl, combine cherry tomatoes, cucumber, red onion, feta cheese, Kalamata olives, and fresh basil.
2. In a small bowl, whisk together extra-virgin olive oil and red wine vinegar to create the dressing.
3. Drizzle the dressing over the salad and toss gently to coat all ingredients evenly.
4. Season with salt and pepper according to your taste preference.

5. Allow the salad to marinate for at least 15 minutes to let the flavors meld.

Cooking Time:
- Preparation: 15 minutes
- Marination: 15 minutes

Pro Tip:
As the flavors develop over time, feel free to adjust the marination duration based on your preference. Longer marination intensifies the taste, providing a more robust and flavorful salad. Watch as the vibrant colors and fresh ingredients come together, creating a sun-kissed dish perfect for any occasion. Enjoy the process and tailor the marination to suit your taste buds!

CHAPTER 19: HEARTY SOUPS - CREAMY ALMOND AND GARLIC SOUP

Ingredients:
- 1 cup almonds, blanched and slivered
- 6 cloves garlic, minced
- 1 onion, finely chopped
  2 tablespoons olive oil
- 4 cups vegetable or chicken broth
- 1 cup potatoes, peeled and diced
- 1 cup leeks, sliced
- 1 teaspoon thyme, dried
- Salt and pepper to taste
- 1 cup heavy cream
- Fresh parsley for garnish

Cooking Time: 30 minutes

Steps:
1. In a dry pan, lightly toast the slivered almonds over medium heat until golden brown. Set aside a handful for garnish.

2. In a large pot, heat olive oil over medium heat. Sauté the chopped onion and minced garlic until softened and aromatic.

3. Add the diced potatoes and sliced leeks to the pot. Stir and cook for an additional 5 minutes until the vegetables begin to soften.

4. Pour in the vegetable or chicken broth, ensuring it covers the vegetables. Season with thyme, salt, and pepper. Bring the mixture to a gentle boil, then reduce the heat and simmer for 15 minutes or until the potatoes are tender.

5. Meanwhile, use a blender to finely grind the toasted almonds. Add the ground almonds to the soup, stirring well.

6. Using an immersion blender or transferring in batches to a regular blender, blend the soup until smooth and creamy.

7. Return the soup to the heat and stir in the heavy cream. Simmer for an additional 5 minutes, allowing the flavors to meld.

8. Adjust seasoning to taste. Serve hot, garnished with the reserved toasted almonds and fresh parsley.

Pro Prompt: Cooking times may vary based on stove efficiency and ingredient sizes. Be attentive to the texture of the potatoes to gauge doneness. For a visual guide, check out our video tutorial online!

CHAPTER 20: TANTALIZING TARTS

Ingredients:
- 1 sheet of puff pastry, thawed
- 1 cup cherry tomatoes, halved
- 1 cup crumbled goat cheese
- 1/4 cup fresh basil, thinly sliced
- 2 tablespoons balsamic glaze
- Salt and pepper to taste

Cooking Time:
- Preparation: 10 minutes
- Cooking: 20 minutes
- Total Time: 30 minutes

Steps:
1. Preheat your oven to 400°F (200°C).

2. Roll out the thawed puff pastry sheet on a lightly floured surface to fit your tart pan.

3. Transfer the rolled-out pastry to the tart pan, pressing it gently into the edges.

4. Prick the pastry with a fork to prevent it from puffing up too much during baking.

5. Spread the crumbled goat cheese evenly over the pastry.

6. Arrange the halved cherry tomatoes on top of the cheese.

7. Season with salt and pepper to taste.

8. Place the tart in the preheated oven and bake for approximately 20 minutes or until the pastry is golden brown and the tomatoes are roasted.

9. Once out of the oven, sprinkle the fresh basil over the tart.

10. Drizzle the balsamic glaze over the tart for a delightful finish.

Pro Tip:
Keep an eye on the tart during the last few minutes of baking, as oven temperatures may vary. Adjust cooking time accordingly for the perfect golden crust and roasted tomatoes.

CHAPTER 21: MEDITERRANEAN MEZZE PLATTER

Ingredients:
- 1 cup Hummus
- 1 cup Stuffed Grape Leaves
- 1 cup Tzatziki Sauce
- 1 cup Marinated Artichoke Hearts

Steps:

1. Hummus with Smoked Paprika:
   - Spread store-bought or homemade hummus on a serving plate.
   - Sprinkle smoked paprika generously over the hummus.
   - Drizzle olive oil on top for extra richness.

2. Stuffed Grape Leaves with Herbed Rice:
   - Arrange stuffed grape leaves on the platter.
   - If using canned grape leaves, drain and pat them dry.
   - Optionally, garnish with fresh dill or a squeeze of lemon.

3. Quick Tzatziki Sauce:

- Mix Greek yogurt, grated cucumber, minced garlic, chopped fresh dill, and a dash of lemon juice.
- Refrigerate for at least 15 minutes before serving.
- Adjust consistency with yogurt if needed.

4. Marinated Artichoke Hearts:
- Drain marinated artichoke hearts and arrange them on the platter.
- Drizzle a bit of the marinade over the artichokes for extra flavor.
- Garnish with chopped parsley for a burst of color.

Cooking Time:
- Preparation Time: 20 minutes
- Assembly Time: 10 minutes

Pro Prompt:
Assemble this Mediterranean Mezze Platter in just 30 minutes! However, keep in mind that preparation times may vary based on individual preferences and cooking experience. Feel free to customize the recipes to your liking and enjoy the process. Consider it a delightful culinary journey with flexible timings.

CHAPTER 22: SPEEDY SEAFOOD SKEWERS

Ingredients:
- 1 lb large shrimp, peeled and deveined
- 1/2 lb chorizo, sliced into rounds
- 1 lb sea scallops
- 1 lemon, sliced
- 2 tablespoons olive oil
- 2 cloves garlic, minced
- 1 teaspoon smoked paprika
- Salt and pepper to taste
- Wooden skewers, soaked in water

Preparation Time: 15 minutes
Cooking Time: 10 minutes
Total Time:25 minutes

Steps:

1. Preheat the Grill: If using an outdoor grill, preheat it to medium-high heat.

2. Prepare the Marinade: In a bowl, combine olive oil, minced garlic, smoked paprika, salt, and pepper. Mix well.

3. Thread the Skewers: Alternate threading shrimp, chorizo slices, sea scallops, and lemon slices onto the soaked wooden skewers.

4. Marinate the Skewers: Brush the skewers generously with the prepared marinade, ensuring even coating on all sides. Let them marinate for about 10 minutes.

5. Grill the Skewers: Place the skewers on the preheated grill and cook for approximately 5 minutes per side or until the shrimp turn opaque and the scallops are cooked through.

6. Baste with Lemon: While grilling, baste the skewers with extra lemon slices for added flavor.

7. Serve Hot: Remove the skewers from the grill and serve immediately. Garnish with fresh herbs if desired.

Pro Tip: Cooking times may vary depending on your grill and the size of the seafood. Keep an eye on the skewers and adjust cooking times accordingly. For an extra burst of flavor, squeeze fresh lemon juice over the skewers just before serving.

30-Minute Andalusian Cookbook

CHAPTER 23: SPANISH-INSPIRED GRAINS

Ingredients:
- 1 cup quinoa
- 2 cups vegetable broth
- 1 pinch of saffron threads
- 1 tablespoon olive oil
- 1 small onion, finely chopped
- 2 cloves garlic, minced
- 1 red bell pepper, diced
- 1 zucchini, diced
- 1 cup cherry tomatoes, halved
- Salt and pepper to taste
- Fresh parsley for garnish

Cooking Time: Approximately 25 minutes

Steps:

1. Prepare the Quinoa:
   - Rinse 1 cup of quinoa under cold water.
   - In a saucepan, combine quinoa, vegetable broth, and a pinch of saffron threads.

- Bring to a boil, then reduce heat, cover, and simmer for 15 minutes or until quinoa is cooked and liquid is absorbed.

2. Sauté the Vegetables:
   - In a large skillet, heat 1 tablespoon of olive oil over medium heat.
   - Add finely chopped onion and minced garlic, sauté until fragrant.
   - Add diced red bell pepper, zucchini, and cherry tomatoes. Cook until vegetables are tender, about 5-7 minutes.

3. Combine and Season:
   - Gently fold the saffron-infused quinoa into the skillet with sautéed vegetables.
   - Season with salt and pepper to taste.

4. Finish and Garnish:
   - Allow the flavors to meld for a few minutes on low heat.
   - Garnish with fresh parsley before serving.

Pro Tip
Feel free to customize the recipe with your favorite vegetables or add a protein of your choice for a heartier meal. Cooking times may vary, so keep an eye on the quinoa and adjust accordingly.

Watch closely as this dish comes together beautifully in just about 25 minutes, but your stovetop intensity may impact the cooking time.

CHAPTER 24: TEMPTING TIRAMISU VARIATIONS

Chocolate Tiramisu

Ingredients:
- 1 cup strong brewed coffee, cooled
- 3 tablespoons cocoa powder
- 250g mascarpone cheese
- 1 cup heavy cream
- 1 cup powdered sugar
- 1 teaspoon vanilla extract
- 24 ladyfinger cookies
- Dark chocolate shavings for garnish

Steps:
1. In a shallow dish, combine brewed coffee and 2 tablespoons of cocoa powder. Set aside.
2. In a mixing bowl, whip the heavy cream until stiff peaks form.
3. In a separate bowl, whisk together mascarpone cheese, powdered sugar, and vanilla extract until smooth.
4. Gently fold the whipped cream into the mascarpone mixture until well combined.

5. Dip each ladyfinger into the coffee mixture, ensuring they are soaked but not overly soggy.
6. Arrange a layer of soaked ladyfingers in the bottom of a serving dish.
7. Spread half of the mascarpone mixture over the ladyfingers.
8. Repeat the layers with remaining ladyfingers and mascarpone mixture.
9. Cover and refrigerate for at least 4 hours or overnight to allow flavors to meld.
10. Before serving, dust the top with the remaining cocoa powder and garnish with dark chocolate shavings.

Cooking Time: 4 hours (including chilling time)

Pro Tip: Keep an eye on the texture of the mascarpone mixture as you fold in the whipped cream—it should be velvety and light. Chilling time may vary, so adjust according to your desired consistency. For an extra indulgence, try experimenting with different cocoa brands for unique flavor profiles. Enjoy this chocolatey twist on the classic Tiramisu!

CHAPTER 25: DECADENT CHOCOLATE CREATIONS

Recipe: Chocolaty Churro Fondue

Ingredients:
- 1 cup dark chocolate, chopped
- 1/2 cup milk chocolate, chopped
- 1 cup heavy cream
- 1 teaspoon vanilla extract
- 1/2 teaspoon ground cinnamon
- 1/4 teaspoon cayenne pepper (optional for a spicy kick)
- Churros for dipping (store-bought or homemade)

Steps:
1. In a saucepan over medium heat, combine the dark chocolate, milk chocolate, and heavy cream.
2. Stir continuously until the chocolates are fully melted and the mixture is smooth.
3. Add vanilla extract, ground cinnamon, and cayenne pepper (if using). Stir well to combine.
4. Once the fondue is velvety and well-blended, remove from heat and transfer to a serving bowl.

Time to Cook:
- Preparation: 10 minutes
- Cooking: 10 minutes
- Total: 20 minutes

Pro Prompt:
Feel free to get creative with your dippables! While traditional churros are fantastic, try dipping pretzels, marshmallows, or even fresh fruit into this luscious chocolate fondue. Keep an eye on the clock, as the cooking time may vary based on your stove's heat and the consistency you desire for the fondue. Enjoy this indulgent treat at your own pace!

CHAPTER 26: MANGO GAZPACHO DELIGHT

Ingredients:
- 4 ripe mangoes, peeled and diced
- 1 cucumber, peeled and chopped
- 1 red bell pepper, diced
- 1 small red onion, finely chopped
- 2 cloves garlic, minced
- 3 cups tomato juice
- 1/4 cup red wine vinegar
- 1/4 cup extra-virgin olive oil
- Salt and pepper to taste
- Fresh cilantro for garnish

Steps:
1. In a blender, combine diced mangoes, cucumber, red bell pepper, red onion, and minced garlic.
2. Add tomato juice, red wine vinegar, and olive oil to the blender.
3. Blend until the mixture is smooth and well combined.
4. Season with salt and pepper to taste. Refrigerate the gazpacho for at least 30 minutes to allow the flavors to meld.

5. Before serving, give the gazpacho a good stir. Ladle it into bowls.

6. Garnish with fresh cilantro and an extra drizzle of olive oil if desired.

Cooking Time: 30 minutes (plus additional chilling time)

Pro Tip: The longer you let the gazpacho chill in the refrigerator, the more intense and delicious the flavors become. Consider preparing it in advance and allowing it to chill for a few hours or even overnight for an extra burst of taste. Remember, the timing can vary, so feel free to adjust based on your preference for flavor intensity.

CHAPTER 27: IRRESISTIBLE RASPBERRY ALMOND TART

Ingredients:
- 1 1/2 cups all-purpose flour
- 1/2 cup almond flour
- 1/2 cup unsalted butter, chilled and cubed
- 1/4 cup granulated sugar
- 1/4 teaspoon salt
- 1 large egg yolk
- 1-2 tablespoons ice water

Filling:
- 1 cup fresh raspberries
- 1/2 cup raspberry jam
- 1 cup almond meal
- 1/2 cup granulated sugar
- 1/4 teaspoon almond extract
- 1/2 cup unsalted butter, melted
- 2 large eggs

Optional:
- Sliced almonds for garnish

- Powdered sugar for dusting

Steps:

1. Prepare the Crust:
   - In a food processor, combine all-purpose flour, almond flour, sugar, and salt.
   - Add chilled butter cubes and pulse until the mixture resembles coarse crumbs.
   - Mix in the egg yolk and gradually add ice water until the dough comes together.
   - Form the dough into a disk, wrap in plastic, and refrigerate for at least 30 minutes.

2. Preheat and Roll:
   - Preheat your oven to 375°F (190°C).
   - Roll out the chilled dough on a floured surface and transfer it to a tart pan, pressing it into the bottom and up the sides. Trim any excess.

3. Blind Bake:
   - Line the crust with parchment paper and fill with pie weights or dried beans.
   - Bake the crust for 15 minutes, then remove the weights and bake for an additional 5 minutes until lightly golden.

4. Prepare the Filling:

- In a bowl, mix almond meal, sugar, melted butter, almond extract, and eggs until well combined.

5. Assemble the Tart:
   - Spread raspberry jam evenly over the pre-baked crust.
   - Pour the almond filling on top, smoothing it with a spatula.
   - Arrange fresh raspberries on the filling.

6. Bake to Perfection:
   - Bake the tart at 350°F (175°C) for 25-30 minutes or until the filling is set and golden brown.

7. Garnish and Serve:
   - Allow the tart to cool before garnishing with sliced almonds and a dusting of powdered sugar.
   - Serve slices at room temperature.

Cooking Time:
- Preparation: 20 minutes
- Chilling: 30 minutes
- Baking: 25-30 minutes

Pro Tip:

Timings may vary based on your oven, so keep an eye on the tart during the last few minutes of baking. Enjoy watching it transform into a delectable masterpiece!

CHAPTER 28: CITRUS BURST AVOCADO SALAD

Ingredients:
- 2 ripe avocados, sliced
- 1 grapefruit, segmented
- 1 orange, segmented
- 1 cup cherry tomatoes, halved
- 1/4 red onion, thinly sliced
- 1/4 cup fresh cilantro, chopped
- 2 tablespoons olive oil
- 1 tablespoon balsamic vinegar
- Salt and pepper to taste

Cooking Time:
- Preparation: 15 minutes
- Total Time: 15 minutes

Instructions:

1. Prepare the Citrus:
   - Peel and segment the grapefruit and orange over a bowl to catch any juices.

2. Assemble the Salad:

- In a large serving bowl, combine the sliced avocados, grapefruit segments, orange segments, halved cherry tomatoes, red onion slices, and chopped cilantro.

3. Whisk the Dressing
- In a small bowl, whisk together the olive oil, balsamic vinegar, and a pinch of salt and pepper.

4. Drizzle and Toss:
- Drizzle the dressing over the salad ingredients. Gently toss the salad to coat everything evenly.

5. Serve Fresh:
- Serve immediately, ensuring each portion has a balanced mix of citrus, avocado, and tomatoes.

Pro Prompt:

Note: Avocado salads are best enjoyed immediately for optimal freshness and texture. Depending on your slicing speed and kitchen efficiency, your preparation time may vary. For a perfect citrus burst, consider preparing the ingredients right before serving. Bon appétit!

CHAPTER 29: SMOKY SPANISH EGGPLANT TAPENADE

Ingredients:
- 2 large eggplants, peeled and diced
- 3 cloves garlic, minced
- 1 red bell pepper, finely chopped
  1/4 cup black olives, sliced
- 2 tablespoons capers
- 1 tablespoon red wine vinegar
- 3 tablespoons extra virgin olive oil
- 1 teaspoon smoked paprika
- Salt and pepper to taste
- Fresh parsley for garnish

Steps:

1. Prepare the Eggplants:
  - Preheat your oven to 400°F (200°C).
  - Spread the diced eggplants on a baking sheet and roast for 20 minutes or until tender.

2. **Sauté Garlic and Bell Pepper:**

- In a skillet over medium heat, sauté minced
garlic and chopped red bell pepper in 2
tablespoons of olive oil until softened.

3. Combine Ingredients:
- In a bowl, combine the roasted eggplants,
sautéed garlic and bell pepper, sliced olives,
capers, red wine vinegar, smoked paprika, salt,
and pepper.

4. Blend to Perfection:
- Using a food processor, blend the mixture
until you achieve a chunky tapenade consistency.

5. Adjust Seasoning:
- Taste the tapenade and adjust salt, pepper, or
smoked paprika to suit your preferences.

6. Chill and Infuse Flavors:
- Let the tapenade chill in the refrigerator for
at least 30 minutes to allow the flavors to meld.

7. Serve with Finesse:
- Drizzle the remaining olive oil over the
tapenade before serving.
- Garnish with fresh parsley for a burst of color
and freshness.

Cooking Time: Approximately 30 minutes

Pro Prompt:
Each kitchen is its own universe, and cooking times may vary. Embrace the culinary journey, tasting as you go, and savor the art of creating a dish uniquely yours.

CHAPTER 30: MEDITERRANEAN STUFFED BELL PEPPERS

Ingredients:
- 4 large bell peppers (any color)
- 1 cup cooked quinoa
- 1 can (15 oz) chickpeas, drained and rinsed
- 1 cup cherry tomatoes, diced
- 1/2 cup feta cheese, crumbled
- 1/4 cup Kalamata olives, chopped
- 2 cloves garlic, minced
- 2 tablespoons olive oil
- 1 teaspoon dried oregano
- Salt and pepper to taste

Steps:
1. Preheat the oven to 375°F (190°C).

2. Cut the tops off the bell peppers and remove seeds and membranes.

3. In a large bowl, combine cooked quinoa, chickpeas, cherry tomatoes, feta cheese, olives, garlic, olive oil, dried oregano, salt, and pepper. Mix well.

4. Stuff each bell pepper with the quinoa mixture, pressing down gently to pack it.

5. Place the stuffed peppers in a baking dish, and drizzle a bit of olive oil over the tops.

6. Bake in the preheated oven for 25-30 minutes or until the peppers are tender.

7. Optional: Broil for an additional 3-5 minutes to get a golden brown top.

Cooking Time:
- Preparation: 15 minutes
- Baking: 25-30 minutes

Pro Tip:
Watch the oven closely during the last few minutes of baking, as cooking times may vary based on individual appliances and variations in pepper size. Achieving the perfect tenderness ensures a delightful dining experience. Enjoy your culinary adventure!

CHAPTER 31: TEMPTING TIRAMISU VARIATIONS - CHOCOLATE TIRAMISU

Ingredients:
- 1 cup strong brewed coffee, cooled
- 3 tablespoons coffee liqueur
- 4 large egg yolks
- 3/4 cup granulated sugar
- 1 cup mascarpone cheese, softened
- 1 cup heavy cream
- 1 teaspoon vanilla extract
- 8 ounces ladyfinger cookies
- 1/4 cup cocoa powder, for dusting

Steps:
1. In a shallow dish, combine the brewed coffee and coffee liqueur. Set aside.

2. In a heatproof bowl, whisk together the egg yolks and granulated sugar. Place the bowl over a pot of simmering water, creating a double boiler. Whisk continuously until the mixture is pale and slightly thickened.

3. Remove the bowl from heat and let it cool slightly. Add the mascarpone cheese and mix until smooth.

4. In a separate bowl, whip the heavy cream and vanilla extract until stiff peaks form. Gently fold the whipped cream into the mascarpone mixture until well combined.

5. Dip each ladyfinger into the coffee mixture for a few seconds, ensuring they are soaked but not overly saturated.

6. In the bottom of a serving dish, arrange a layer of soaked ladyfingers.

7. Spread half of the mascarpone mixture over the ladyfingers, creating an even layer.

8. Repeat the process with another layer of soaked ladyfingers and the remaining mascarpone mixture.

9. Cover and refrigerate the tiramisu for at least 4 hours or overnight to allow the flavors to meld.

10. Before serving, sift cocoa powder over the top for a finishing touch.

Cooking Time:
– Preparation: 30 minutes
– Refrigeration: 4 hours or overnight

Pro Tip:
Watch the clock, as the refrigeration time can vary. The longer it chills, the more exquisite the flavors become. Patience is a sweet reward in the world of tiramisu!

CHAPTER 32: CITRUS AVOCADO SALAD

Ingredients:
- 2 ripe avocados, sliced
- 1 grapefruit, peeled and segmented
- 2 oranges, peeled and segmented
- 1 red onion, thinly sliced
- 1/4 cup fresh cilantro, chopped
- 2 tablespoons extra virgin olive oil
- 1 tablespoon balsamic vinegar
- Salt and pepper to taste

Cooking Time:
- Preparation: 15 minutes
- Total Time: 15 minutes

Instructions:
1. **Prepare the Citrus:** Peel and segment the grapefruit and oranges. Ensure to remove any seeds.

2. **Slice Avocados:** Cut the avocados in half, remove the pit, and slice the flesh into thin, elegant slices.

3. **Thinly Slice Red Onion:**** Peel and thinly slice the red onion to add a hint of sharpness.

4. **Assemble the Salad:** In a large bowl, gently combine the avocado slices, citrus segments, and sliced red onion.

5. **Add Cilantro:** Sprinkle freshly chopped cilantro over the mixture for a burst of freshness.

6. **Prepare the Dressing:** In a small bowl, whisk together extra virgin olive oil and balsamic vinegar. Season with salt and pepper to taste.

7. **Drizzle Dressing:** Pour the dressing over the salad, ensuring an even coat. Gently toss to combine.

8. **Serve Immediately:** This salad is best enjoyed fresh. Serve immediately and savor the vibrant flavors.

Pro Tip:
Timing may vary based on the ripeness of avocados and citrus fruits. For optimal taste, prepare the dressing just before serving. Enjoy this refreshing salad on its own or as a delightful side dish.

CHAPTER 33: CITRUS BLISS TART

Ingredients:
- 1 ½ cups all-purpose flour
- ½ cup unsalted butter, chilled and cubed
- ¼ cup powdered sugar
- 1 large egg yolk
- 2 tablespoons ice water

For the Filling:
- 1 cup fresh orange juice
- Zest of 2 oranges
- ½ cup granulated sugar
- 3 tablespoons cornstarch
- 4 large egg yolks
- ¼ cup unsalted butter

For the Garnish:
- Fresh orange slices
- Mint leaves

Steps:

For the Crust:

1. In a food processor, pulse together flour, powdered sugar, and chilled butter until the mixture resembles coarse crumbs.
2. Add the egg yolk and pulse until the dough starts to come together.
3. Gradually add ice water, one tablespoon at a time, pulsing until the dough forms a ball.
4. Flatten the dough into a disc, wrap in plastic, and refrigerate for 30 minutes.
5. Preheat the oven to 375°F (190°C).
6. Roll out the chilled dough on a floured surface and press it into a tart pan. Trim excess dough.
7. Bake the crust for 15 minutes or until golden brown. Let it cool completely.

For the Filling:

8. In a saucepan, whisk together orange juice, orange zest, sugar, cornstarch, and egg yolks over medium heat.
9. Continue whisking until the mixture thickens, around 5-7 minutes.
10. Remove from heat and stir in butter until smooth.
11. Pour the filling into the cooled tart crust and spread it evenly.
12. Refrigerate for at least 2 hours or until set.

Garnish:

13. Before serving, decorate with fresh orange slices and mint leaves.

Cooking Time:
- Preparation: 20 minutes
- Crust Baking: 15 minutes
- Filling Preparation: 10 minutes
- Refrigeration: 2 hours

Pro Tip:
Each oven varies, so keep an eye on the crust during baking. Also, chilling times may vary depending on your refrigerator. Enjoy the process and savor the citrusy delight!

CHAPTER 34: CITRUS-INFUSED TIRAMISU CUPS

Ingredients:
- 1 cup strong brewed coffee, cooled
- 3 tablespoons orange liqueur
- 4 large egg yolks
- 3/4 cup granulated sugar
- 1 cup mascarpone cheese
- 1 cup heavy cream
- 1 teaspoon vanilla extract
- Zest of 1 orange
- 24 ladyfinger cookies
- Dark chocolate shavings for garnish
- Fresh mint leaves for garnish

Steps:
1. In a shallow dish, combine the brewed coffee and orange liqueur. Set aside.

2. In a heatproof bowl, whisk together egg yolks and sugar. Place the bowl over a pot of simmering water (double boiler) and whisk continuously until the mixture thickens.

3. Remove from heat and let it cool slightly. Add mascarpone cheese and mix until smooth.

4. In a separate bowl, whip the heavy cream until stiff peaks form. Gently fold the whipped cream into the mascarpone mixture.

5. Stir in vanilla extract and orange zest, ensuring a well-incorporated, velvety texture.

6. Briefly dip each ladyfinger into the coffee mixture, ensuring they are moistened but not overly soaked.

7. In serving cups or glasses, layer the soaked ladyfingers with the mascarpone mixture, creating alternating layers.

8. Repeat until you reach the top, finishing with a layer of the mascarpone mixture.

9. Refrigerate for at least 4 hours or overnight to allow the flavors to meld.

10. Before serving, garnish with dark chocolate shavings and fresh mint leaves.

Cooking Time:

- Prep Time: 20 minutes
- Chilling Time: 4 hours minimum

Pro Tip:
Watch the clock as you whip up this delightful
dessert! Chilling times may vary based on your
refrigerator and personal preferences. The longer
it chills, the more the flavors meld, so feel free to
prepare it ahead for an even more indulgent
experience.

Chapter 35: Speedy Saffron Quinoa

Ingredients:
- 1 cup quinoa, rinsed and drained
- 2 cups vegetable broth
- 1/4 teaspoon saffron threads
- 1 tablespoon olive oil
- 1 small onion, finely chopped
- 2 cloves garlic, minced
- 1/2 teaspoon ground cumin
- Salt and pepper to taste
- Chopped fresh parsley for garnish

Cooking Time: 30 minutes

Steps:
1. Prepare the Saffron Infusion:
   - In a small bowl, combine saffron threads with 2 tablespoons of hot water. Allow it to steep and infuse while you prepare the quinoa.

2. Sauté Aromatics:
   - Heat olive oil in a medium saucepan over medium heat. Add chopped onion and sauté until

translucent. Add minced garlic and cook for an additional minute.

3. Toast Quinoa:
- Add rinsed quinoa to the saucepan, stirring frequently to toast it slightly for about 2-3 minutes.

4. Enhance with Saffron:
- Pour in the saffron infusion, stirring well to evenly distribute the saffron's vibrant color and flavor throughout the quinoa.

5. Season and Simmer:
- Season with ground cumin, salt, and pepper. Pour in vegetable broth and bring the mixture to a boil. Once boiling, reduce heat to low, cover, and simmer for 15-18 minutes or until quinoa is cooked and liquid is absorbed.

6. Fluff and Garnish:
- Remove the saucepan from heat, let it sit covered for 5 minutes. Fluff the quinoa with a fork and sprinkle with chopped fresh parsley.

Pro Prompt for Readers:

Cooking times may vary based on stove intensity and altitude. Keep an eye on the quinoa and adjust the simmering time accordingly. Enjoy experimenting with this quick and flavorful dish!

Chapter 36: Mediterranean Stuffed Bell Peppers

Ingredients
- 4 large bell peppers (any color)
- 1 cup quinoa, cooked
- 1 can (15 oz) chickpeas, drained and rinsed
- 1 cup cherry tomatoes, diced
- 1/2 cup Kalamata olives, chopped
- 1/2 cup feta cheese, crumbled
- 2 cloves garlic, minced
- 1 teaspoon dried oregano
- 1 teaspoon dried basil
- Salt and pepper to taste
- 2 tablespoons olive oil
- Fresh parsley for garnish

Cooking Time:
- Preparation: 15 minutes
- Cooking: 25 minutes
- Total Time: 40 minutes

Cooking Instructions:
1. Preheat the oven to 375°F (190°C).

2. Cut the tops off the bell peppers and remove the seeds and membranes. Lightly brush the outside of the peppers with olive oil and place them in a baking dish.

3. In a large bowl, mix together the cooked quinoa, chickpeas, cherry tomatoes, olives, feta cheese, minced garlic, dried oregano, dried basil, salt, and pepper.

4. Stuff each bell pepper with the quinoa mixture, pressing down gently to pack the filling.

5. Drizzle the stuffed peppers with olive oil and replace the tops.

6. Cover the baking dish with foil and bake for 20 minutes. Then, remove the foil and bake for an additional 5 minutes or until the peppers are tender.

7. Garnish with fresh parsley before serving.

Pro Tip for Readers:
Cooking times may vary based on your oven and the size of the peppers. Keep an eye on them during the last few minutes of baking to ensure they reach your desired level of tenderness. Enjoy these Mediterranean Stuffed Bell Peppers as a delightful and customizable dish!

CHAPTER 37: LEMON HERB BAKED COD

Ingredients:
- 4 cod fillets
- 2 tablespoons olive oil
- 1 lemon, thinly sliced
- 3 cloves garlic, minced
- 1 teaspoon dried thyme
- 1 teaspoon dried rosemary
- Salt and pepper to taste
- Fresh parsley for garnish

Cooking Time: 30 minutes

Instructions:

1. Preheat your oven to 400°F (200°C).

2. Place the cod fillets on a baking sheet lined with parchment paper.

3. Drizzle olive oil over the cod fillets, ensuring they are well-coated.

4. Sprinkle minced garlic, dried thyme, dried rosemary, salt, and pepper evenly over each fillet.

5. Arrange lemon slices on top of the cod fillets for a burst of citrus flavor.

6. Bake in the preheated oven for 15-20 minutes or until the cod is opaque and easily flakes with a fork.

7. For a golden finish, broil the cod for an additional 2-3 minutes.

8. Garnish with fresh parsley before serving.

Pro Tip: Cooking times may vary depending on your oven and the thickness of the cod fillets. Keep a close eye on the dish to ensure the fish is perfectly cooked.

CHAPTER 38: SPEEDY SAFFRON QUINOA

Ingredients:
- 1 cup quinoa
- 2 cups vegetable broth
- 1/4 teaspoon saffron threads
- 1 tablespoon olive oil
- 1/4 cup finely chopped onion
- 2 cloves garlic, minced
- 1/2 cup diced bell pepper (any color)
- 1/2 cup diced tomatoes
- Salt and pepper to taste
- Fresh parsley for garnish

Cooking Time: 30 minutes

Steps:
1. Rinse the quinoa under cold water, then combine it with vegetable broth in a saucepan. Add saffron threads and bring to a boil.
2. Once boiling, reduce the heat to low, cover, and let it simmer for 15-20 minutes or until the quinoa is cooked and the liquid is absorbed.

3. In a separate skillet, heat olive oil over medium heat. Add chopped onion and garlic, sauté until softened.

4. Add diced bell pepper to the skillet and cook for an additional 3-4 minutes until the peppers are slightly tender.

5. Stir in the diced tomatoes and continue cooking for another 2-3 minutes.

6. Once the quinoa is ready, fluff it with a fork and add it to the skillet with the vegetable mixture. Mix well.

7. Season with salt and pepper to taste. Allow the flavors to meld for 2-3 minutes on low heat.

8. Garnish with fresh parsley before serving.

Pro Tip: Cooking times may vary, ensure the quinoa is fluffy and fully cooked before combining with the sautéed vegetables. Watch the clock but trust your senses for the perfect texture. Enjoy this versatile dish as a side or a nutritious main course!

CHAPTER 39: SEASIDE SERENITY - GRILLED GARLIC SHRIMP SKEWERS

Ingredients:
- 1 pound large shrimp, peeled and deveined
- 3 cloves garlic, minced
- 2 tablespoons olive oil
- 1 teaspoon smoked paprika
- 1 teaspoon cayenne pepper (adjust to taste)
- Salt and pepper to taste
- Lemon wedges for garnish
- Fresh parsley, chopped (for garnish)

Cooking Time: Approximately 20 minutes

Preparation Time: 10 minutes

Total Time: 30 minutes

Equipment:
- Grill or grill pan
- Wooden skewers, soaked in water for 30 minutes

Steps:

1. Preheat the Grill:
   - If using a charcoal grill, light the charcoal and let it burn until the coals are covered with white ash. If using a gas grill, preheat it to medium-high heat.

2. Marinate the Shrimp:
   - In a bowl, combine the minced garlic, olive oil, smoked paprika, cayenne pepper, salt, and pepper. Mix well.
   - Add the peeled and deveined shrimp to the marinade, ensuring they are well-coated. Allow the shrimp to marinate for at least 10 minutes to absorb the flavors.

3. Skewer the Shrimp:
   - Thread the marinated shrimp onto the soaked wooden skewers, ensuring they are evenly distributed.

4. Grill the Shrimp:
   - Place the shrimp skewers on the preheated grill and cook for approximately 2-3 minutes per side or until the shrimp turn pink and opaque. Be

cautious not to overcook to maintain a juicy texture.

5. Garnish and Serve:
- Remove the shrimp skewers from the grill and transfer them to a serving platter.
- Garnish with freshly chopped parsley and serve with lemon wedges on the side for a burst of citrus freshness.

Pro Tip for Readers:
Cooking times may vary depending on your grill's heat intensity. Keep a close eye on the shrimp, and adjust cooking times accordingly. For a perfect sear, resist the temptation to flip them too soon. Enjoy this seaside-inspired dish with family and friends while savoring the delightful moments around the grill.

CHAPTER 40: SPICY SAFFRON RICE PILAF

Ingredients:
- 1 cup Basmati rice
- 2 cups vegetable broth
- 1 tablespoon olive oil
- 1 small onion, finely chopped
- 2 cloves garlic, minced
- 1 teaspoon ground cumin
- 1/2 teaspoon smoked paprika
- 1/4 teaspoon saffron threads, soaked in 2 tablespoons warm water
- Salt and pepper to taste
- 1/4 cup chopped fresh cilantro for garnish

Cooking Time: 30 minutes

Servings: 4

Instructions:

1. Rinse the Basmati rice under cold water until the water runs clear. Drain and set aside.

2. In a medium saucepan, heat the olive oil over medium heat. Add the chopped onion and sauté until translucent, about 3-4 minutes.

3. Add the minced garlic to the onions and sauté for an additional 1-2 minutes until fragrant.

4. Stir in the cumin and smoked paprika, coating the onions and garlic in the spices.

5. Add the rinsed Basmati rice to the saucepan, stirring to combine with the onion and spice mixture.

6. Pour in the vegetable broth and the saffron-infused water. Season with salt and pepper to taste.

7. Bring the mixture to a boil, then reduce the heat to low, cover the saucepan with a tight-fitting lid, and simmer for 15-18 minutes or until the rice is tender and the liquid is absorbed.

8. Once cooked, fluff the rice with a fork and let it sit, covered, for an additional 5 minutes to allow the flavors to meld.

9. Garnish the spicy saffron rice pilaf with chopped cilantro before serving.

Pro Tip for Readers:
The cooking time may vary based on your stove and the specific rice you use. Keep an eye on the rice starting around the 15-minute mark to ensure it doesn't overcook. Adjust the simmering time accordingly for the perfect fluffy texture. Enjoy experimenting and savoring the aromatic flavors!

CHAPTER 41: CITRUS-INFUSED SALMON SKEWERS

Ingredients:
- 1 lb fresh salmon fillets, cubed
- 2 lemons, zested and juiced
- 1 orange, zested and juiced
- 3 tablespoons olive oil
- 2 cloves garlic, minced
- 1 teaspoon smoked paprika
- Salt and pepper to taste
- Wooden skewers, soaked in water for 30 minutes

Cooking Time:
- Marination: 20 minutes
- Grilling: 10 minutes

Cooking Steps:

1. Prepare the Marinade:
   - In a bowl, combine lemon zest, lemon juice, orange zest, orange juice, olive oil, minced garlic, smoked paprika, salt, and pepper. Whisk until well combined.

2. Marinate the Salmon:

- Place the salmon cubes in a shallow dish. Pour the marinade over the salmon, ensuring each piece is coated. Allow it to marinate in the refrigerator for at least 20 minutes.

3. Skewer the Salmon:

- Preheat the grill to medium-high heat. Thread the marinated salmon cubes onto the soaked wooden skewers.

4. Grill the Skewers:

- Grill the salmon skewers for approximately 5 minutes per side, or until the salmon is cooked through and has a delightful char.

5. Serve and Enjoy:

- Remove the skewers from the grill and serve the citrus-infused salmon skewers hot. Garnish with additional lemon and orange zest if desired.

Pro Tip for Readers:

*lCooking times may vary based on grill temperature and thickness of salmon. Keep a close eye on the skewers to ensure they are perfectly cooked. Enjoy the cooking process, and don't hesitate to make adjustments based on your preferences!*1

CHAPTER 42: SPANISH HOT CHOCOLATE WITH CHURRO DIPPERS

Ingredients:
- 2 cups whole milk
- 150g high-quality dark chocolate, finely chopped
- 3 tablespoons granulated sugar
- 1 teaspoon vanilla extract
- Pinch of salt
- Churros for dipping (store-bought or homemade)

Cooking Time:
- Preparation: 10 minutes
- Cooking: 10 minutes
- Total: 20 minutes

Instructions:

1. Prepare the Hot Chocolate:
   - In a saucepan over medium heat, warm the milk until it begins to steam but avoid boiling.

- Add the finely chopped dark chocolate to the milk and whisk continuously until the chocolate is fully melted and incorporated.

- Stir in the granulated sugar, vanilla extract, and a pinch of salt. Continue whisking until the mixture is smooth and slightly thickened.

2. Simmer and Serve:

- Allow the hot chocolate to simmer for an additional 5 minutes, ensuring it reaches your desired thickness.

- Taste and adjust sweetness if needed. Remove from heat.

3. Churro Dippers:

- While the hot chocolate is simmering, prepare your churros. You can use store-bought churros or make them from scratch according to the package or recipe instructions.

4. Serve and Enjoy:

- Pour the rich and velvety hot chocolate into mugs.

- Arrange the churros on a plate for dipping.

Pro Tip for Readers:

Watch the simmering carefully as the thickness of the hot chocolate can vary based on personal

preference. Adjust the simmering time to achieve
your desired consistency, whether you prefer a
thick, indulgent hot chocolate or a lighter, more
sippable version. Enjoy this cozy treat at your
own preferred pace!

CHAPTER 44: MEDITERRANEAN STUFFED BELL PEPPERS

Ingredients:
- 4 large bell peppers (any color)
- 1 cup quinoa, rinsed
- 2 cups vegetable broth
- 1 can (15 oz) chickpeas, drained and rinsed
- 1 cup cherry tomatoes, halved
- 1/2 cup Kalamata olives, sliced
- 1/2 cup crumbled feta cheese
- 1/4 cup fresh parsley, chopped
- 2 cloves garlic, minced
- 2 tablespoons olive oil
- 1 teaspoon dried oregano
- Salt and pepper to taste

Cooking Time:
- Prep Time: 15 minutes
- Cook Time: 30 minutes
- Total Time: 45 minutes

Instructions:
1. Preheat the oven to 375°F (190°C).

2. Cut the tops off the bell peppers and remove seeds and membranes. Place them in a baking dish.

3. In a medium saucepan, combine quinoa and vegetable broth. Bring to a boil, then reduce heat, cover, and simmer for 15 minutes or until the quinoa is cooked and the liquid is absorbed.

4. In a large mixing bowl, combine cooked quinoa, chickpeas, cherry tomatoes, Kalamata olives, feta cheese, parsley, garlic, olive oil, dried oregano, salt, and pepper. Mix well.

5. Spoon the quinoa mixture into each bell pepper until they are fully stuffed.

6. Place the stuffed peppers in the preheated oven and bake for 30 minutes or until the peppers are tender.

Pro Tip for Readers:
As oven temperatures may vary, keep an eye on the peppers after 25 minutes. A golden brown top indicates they are ready. Enjoy the aroma and make this dish your own by experimenting with additional herbs or spice variations!

CHAPTER 45: LEMON HERB BAKED COD

Ingredients:
- 4 cod fillets
- 2 lemons (zested and juiced)
- 3 cloves garlic (minced)
- 2 tablespoons fresh parsley (chopped)
- 1 teaspoon dried oregano
- 1/2 teaspoon paprika
- Salt and black pepper to taste
- 3 tablespoons olive oil

Cooking Time:
- Preparation: 10 minutes
- Marination: 15 minutes
- Baking: 20 minutes

Total Time: 45 minutes

Instructions:

1. Preheat the Oven:
  - Preheat your oven to 400°F (200°C).

2. Prepare the Marinade:

- In a bowl, combine lemon zest, lemon juice, minced garlic, chopped parsley, dried oregano, paprika, salt, black pepper, and olive oil. Mix well to create a flavorful marinade.

3. Marinate the Cod:
- Place the cod fillets in a shallow dish. Pour the prepared marinade over the fillets, ensuring they are well-coated. Allow them to marinate for at least 15 minutes to absorb the flavors.

4. Arrange on Baking Sheet:
- Line a baking sheet with parchment paper. Place the marinated cod fillets on the sheet, leaving space between each.

5. Bake to Perfection:
- Bake in the preheated oven for approximately 20 minutes or until the cod is cooked through and flakes easily with a fork. The edges should turn golden.

6. Serve and Enjoy:
- Carefully remove the baked cod from the oven. Serve hot, garnished with additional fresh parsley and lemon wedges if desired.

Pro Tip:

Watch the baking time closely as it may vary depending on the thickness of the cod fillets. For optimal results, use a meat thermometer to ensure the internal temperature reaches 145°F (63°C). Enjoy this delightful dish with your favorite side for a wholesome and flavorful meal!

CHAPTER 46: MEDITERRANEAN STUFFED BELL PEPPERS

Ingredients
- 4 large bell peppers (assorted colors)
- 1 cup cooked quinoa
- 1 cup diced tomatoes
- 1 cup chickpeas, drained and rinsed
- 1/2 cup crumbled feta cheese
- 1/4 cup Kalamata olives, chopped
- 2 cloves garlic, minced
- 1 teaspoon dried oregano
- 1 teaspoon ground cumin
- Salt and pepper to taste
- Olive oil for drizzling

Cooking Time: Approximately 30 minutes

Steps:
1. Preheat your oven to 375°F (190°C).
2. Cut the tops off the bell peppers and remove the seeds and membranes.
3. In a large mixing bowl, combine quinoa, diced tomatoes, chickpeas, feta cheese, Kalamata

olives, minced garlic, dried oregano, ground cumin, salt, and pepper. Mix well.

4. Stuff each bell pepper with the quinoa mixture, pressing it down gently.

5. Place the stuffed peppers in a baking dish and drizzle with olive oil.

6. Bake in the preheated oven for about 25-30 minutes or until the peppers are tender and the filling is heated through.

7. Remove from the oven and let them cool for a few minutes before serving.

Pro Tip for Readers:
As oven temperatures may vary, keep an eye on the peppers towards the end of the cooking time. A perfectly cooked stuffed pepper should have a tender pepper shell and a flavorful, warm filling. Adjust the cooking time accordingly for your specific oven. Enjoy experimenting and savoring the delightful flavors of these Mediterranean Stuffed Bell Peppers!

CHAPTER 47: LEMON HERB BAKED COD

Ingredients:
- 4 cod fillets
- 1 lemon, sliced
- 3 tablespoons olive oil
- 2 cloves garlic, minced
- 1 teaspoon dried thyme
- 1 teaspoon dried rosemary
- Salt and pepper to taste
- Fresh parsley for garnish

Cooking Time:
- Preparation: 10 minutes
- Marination: 15 minutes
- Baking: 20 minutes
- Total Time: 45 minutes

Instructions:
1. Preheat the Oven:
   - Preheat your oven to 375°F (190°C).

2. Prepare the Cod:
   - Pat the cod fillets dry with paper towels.
   - Place the fillets in a baking dish.

3. Season the Cod
 - In a small bowl, mix olive oil, minced garlic, dried thyme, dried rosemary, salt, and pepper.
 - Drizzle the herb mixture over the cod fillets, ensuring they are evenly coated.

4. Add Lemon Slices
 - Place lemon slices on top of each fillet for a burst of citrus flavor.

5. Marinate:
 - Allow the cod to marinate for about 15 minutes, letting the flavors infuse.

6. Bake:
 - Place the baking dish in the preheated oven and bake for approximately 20 minutes or until the cod is opaque and easily flakes with a fork.

7. Garnish and Serve
 - Remove from the oven, garnish with fresh parsley, and serve immediately.

Pro Tip:
Watch the baking time closely as it may vary depending on the thickness of your cod fillets. Adjust accordingly to ensure perfectly baked,

tender cod. Enjoy this delightful dish with a side of your favorite vegetables or a bed of seasoned rice!

CHAPTER 48: SPEEDY SEAFOOD SKEWERS

Ingredients:
- 1 pound large shrimp, peeled and deveined
- 1/2 pound chorizo, sliced into rounds
- 1 lemon, thinly sliced
- 1/4 cup olive oil
- 2 cloves garlic, minced
- 1 teaspoon smoked paprika
- Salt and black pepper to taste
- Wooden skewers, soaked in water for 30 minutes

Cooking Time: 20 minutes

Preparation Time:10 minutes

Total Time: 30 minutes

Steps:2

1. Preheat the Grill:

- If using an outdoor grill, preheat it to medium-high heat. If using an indoor grill pan, set it over medium-high heat.

2. **Marinate the Shrimp:** - In a bowl, combine shrimp, olive oil, minced garlic, smoked paprika, salt, and black pepper. Toss well to coat the shrimp evenly. Let it marinate for at least 10 minutes.

3. **Skewer the Ingredients:**
  - Thread the marinated shrimp, chorizo slices, and lemon slices onto the soaked wooden skewers, alternating between ingredients for a vibrant mix of flavors.

4. **Grill the Skewers:** - Place the skewers on the preheated grill and cook for approximately 5-7 minutes on each side or until the shrimp are opaque and the chorizo is nicely charred.

5. **Baste with Lemon**
  - During the last few minutes of grilling, baste the skewers with fresh lemon juice to enhance the citrusy aroma.

6. **Serve Hot**

- Once cooked, transfer the skewers to a serving platter. Drizzle with extra olive oil if desired and serve hot.

7. Enjoy the Fiesta
- These Speedy Seafood Skewers are perfect for any gathering or a quick weeknight meal. Serve with a side of your favorite dipping sauce and enjoy the burst of Mediterranean flavors!

Pro Tip: Pair these skewers with a refreshing salad or a side of couscous for a complete and delightful meal.

CHAPTER 49: ZESTY LEMON HERB GRILLED CHICKEN

Ingredients:
- 4 boneless, skinless chicken breasts
- 2 lemons, juiced
- 3 tablespoons olive oil
- 2 cloves garlic, minced
- 1 teaspoon dried oregano
- 1 teaspoon dried thyme
- Salt and pepper to taste

Steps:

1. Prepare Marinade:
   - In a bowl, whisk together lemon juice, olive oil, minced garlic, dried oregano, dried thyme, salt, and pepper.

2. Marinate Chicken:
   - Place chicken breasts in a resealable plastic bag or shallow dish. Pour the marinade over the chicken, ensuring each piece is well-coated. Seal the bag or cover the dish and refrigerate for at least 30 minutes.

3. Preheat Grill
  - Preheat your grill to medium-high heat.

4. Grill Chicken:
  - Remove chicken from the marinade and let excess drip off. Grill the chicken for approximately 6-8 minutes per side or until the internal temperature reaches 165°F (74°C).

5. Baste with Marinade
  - While grilling, baste the chicken with some of the remaining marinade to enhance flavor and moisture.

6. Check for Doneness
  - To ensure the chicken is thoroughly cooked, use a meat thermometer to check the internal temperature. The juices should run clear.

7. Rest and Serve
  - Allow the grilled chicken to rest for a few minutes before serving. This helps the juices redistribute for a juicier result.

Cooking Time
  - Marinating Time: 30 minutes

- Grill Time: 12–16 minutes (6–8 minutes per side)

Pro Tip
As grill times may vary, always keep an eye on the chicken and adjust cooking times accordingly. The goal is juicy, flavorful chicken with a perfect char, so be mindful of your specific grill's heat.

CHAPTER 50: SMOKY PAPRIKA DEVILED EGGS

Ingredients:
- 6 hard-boiled eggs
- 3 tablespoons mayonnaise
- 1 teaspoon Dijon mustard
- 1 teaspoon smoked paprika
- 1 tablespoon finely chopped chives
- Salt and pepper to taste
- Smoked paprika and chive sprigs for garnish

Cooking Time: 20 minutes

Steps

1. **Boil the Eggs:**Place eggs in a saucepan and cover with water. Bring to a boil, then reduce heat and simmer for 10 minutes. Transfer eggs to an ice bath to cool, then peel.

2. **Slice and Scoop**: Cut each hard-boiled egg in half lengthwise. Carefully remove the yolks and place them in a bowl.

3. **Prepare the Filling:** Mash the egg yolks with a fork. Add mayonnaise, Dijon mustard, smoked paprika, chopped chives, salt, and pepper. Mix until smooth and well combined.

4. **Fill the Egg Whites** Spoon or pipe the yolk mixture back into the egg white halves.

5. **Garnish:** Sprinkle each deviled egg with a pinch of smoked paprika and top with a chive sprig for a touch of freshness.

Pro Tip: Cooking times may vary, so keep an eye on your eggs while boiling to achieve the perfect consistency. Enjoy these Smoky Paprika Deviled Eggs as a delightful appetizer for any occasion! For a step-by-step visual guide, check out our online video tutorial.

CHAPTER 51: CITRUS-INFUSED TIRAMISU CUPS

Ingredients:
- 1 cup strong brewed espresso, cooled
- 3 tablespoons orange liqueur
- 3 large egg yolks
- 3/4 cup granulated sugar
- 1 cup mascarpone cheese, softened
- 1 cup heavy cream
- 1 teaspoon vanilla extract
- Zest of 1 orange
- 24 to 30 ladyfinger cookies
- Cocoa powder for dusting

Steps:

1. In a shallow bowl, combine the brewed espresso and orange liqueur. Set aside.

2. In a heatproof bowl, whisk together egg yolks and sugar. Place the bowl over a pot of simmering water (double boiler) and whisk constantly until the mixture thickens and

becomes pale in color. Remove from heat and let it cool.

3. In a separate bowl, whip the heavy cream until stiff peaks form.

4. Gently fold the mascarpone cheese into the cooled egg yolk mixture until smooth.

5. Fold in the whipped cream, vanilla extract, and orange zest until well combined.

6. Dip each ladyfinger into the espresso mixture for a few seconds, making sure they are soaked but not soggy.

7. Arrange a layer of soaked ladyfingers at the bottom of serving cups or glasses.

8. Spoon a layer of the mascarpone mixture over the ladyfingers.

9. Repeat the layers, finishing with a layer of the mascarpone mixture on top.

10. Cover and refrigerate for at least 4 hours, or preferably overnight, to allow the flavors to meld and the tiramisu to set.

134

Cooking Time:
- Preparation: 20 minutes
- Chilling: 4 hours or overnight

Pro Prompt for Reader:
Adjust the chilling time based on your preference;
longer chilling enhances the flavors. Feel free to
personalize by adding a sprinkle of cocoa powder
or a garnish of orange zest before serving. Enjoy
your time creating this delightful citrus-infused
treat!

CHAPTER 52: MEDITERRANEAN STUFFED BELL PEPPERS

Ingredients:
- 4 large bell peppers (assorted colors)
- 1 cup cooked quinoa
- 1 can (15 oz) chickpeas, drained and rinsed
- 1 cup cherry tomatoes, halved
- 1/2 cup crumbled feta cheese
- 1/4 cup Kalamata olives, chopped
- 2 tablespoons fresh parsley, chopped
- 2 tablespoons olive oil
- 1 teaspoon dried oregano
- Salt and pepper to taste

Steps:
1. Preheat the oven to 375°F (190°C).

2. Cut the tops off the bell peppers and remove seeds and membranes. Place them in a baking dish.

3. In a large mixing bowl, combine cooked quinoa, chickpeas, cherry tomatoes, feta cheese,

olives, parsley, olive oil, dried oregano, salt, and pepper. Mix well.

4. Stuff each bell pepper with the quinoa mixture, pressing down gently to pack the filling.

5. Place the stuffed peppers in the preheated oven and bake for 25-30 minutes or until the peppers are tender.

6. Remove from the oven and let them cool for a few minutes before serving.

Cooking Time: 25-30 minutes

Pro Prompt for Readers:
Cooking times may vary based on your oven and the size of the peppers. Keep an eye on them, and when the peppers are tender and the filling is heated through, your Mediterranean Stuffed Bell Peppers are ready to delight your taste buds! Enjoy experimenting with your own twists and flavors.

CHAPTER 53: LEMON HERB BAKED COD

Ingredients:
- 4 cod fillets
- 2 lemons, sliced
- 3 tablespoons olive oil
- 2 cloves garlic, minced
- 1 teaspoon dried thyme
- 1 teaspoon dried rosemary
- Salt and pepper to taste
- Fresh parsley, chopped (for garnish)

Cooking Time: Approximately 20 minutes

Difficulty: Easy

Steps:
1. Preheat your oven to 400°F (200°C).
2. Pat the cod fillets dry with paper towels and place them in a baking dish.
3. In a small bowl, mix the olive oil, minced garlic, dried thyme, dried rosemary, salt, and pepper.
4. Drizzle the herb mixture over the cod fillets, ensuring they are well-coated.

5. Place lemon slices on top of each fillet for a burst of citrus flavor.
6. Bake in the preheated oven for about 15–20 minutes or until the cod flakes easily with a fork.
7. Garnish with fresh parsley before serving.

Pro Tip: Cooking times may vary depending on the thickness of your cod fillets. Keep an eye on the fish, and adjust the cooking time accordingly. A fork should easily flake the fish, and it should be opaque throughout when done.

CHAPTER 54: GARLIC ROSEMARY LAMB CHOPS

Ingredients:
- 4 lamb chops
- 3 cloves of garlic, minced
- 2 tablespoons fresh rosemary, finely chopped
- 2 tablespoons olive oil
- Salt and pepper to taste

Cooking Time:
- Preparation: 10 minutes
- Marination: 20 minutes
- Cooking: 15 minutes
- Total Time: 45 minutes

Steps:
1. Prepare the Marinade:
   - In a bowl, combine minced garlic, chopped rosemary, olive oil, salt, and pepper.
   - Mix the ingredients thoroughly to create a flavorful marinade.

2. Marinate the Lamb Chops:

- Rub the marinade over the lamb chops, ensuring they are evenly coated.
- Allow the lamb chops to marinate for at least 20 minutes to absorb the flavors.

3. Preheat the Grill or Pan:

- If using a grill, preheat it to medium-high heat. If using a pan, set it over medium-high heat.

4. Cooking the Lamb Chops:

- Place the marinated lamb chops on the grill or in the pan.
- Cook for approximately 5-7 minutes on each side for medium-rare, adjusting based on your desired doneness.

5. Rest and Serve:

- Allow the lamb chops to rest for a few minutes before serving to retain juices.
- Garnish with additional rosemary if desired and serve.

Pro Tip for Readers:

Watch the cooking time closely, as it may vary based on the thickness of the lamb chops and your preferred level of doneness. Use a meat thermometer for precision, aiming for an internal temperature of 145°F (63°C) for medium-rare lamb. Adjust the cooking time accordingly for a perfect, succulent dish.

CHAPTER 55: SEASIDE DELIGHTS - GRILLED SARDINES WITH LEMON HERB MARINADE

Ingredients:
- 8 fresh sardines, cleaned and gutted
- 1/4 cup olive oil
- 3 tablespoons fresh lemon juice
- 2 cloves garlic, minced
- 2 teaspoons fresh thyme, chopped
- 1 teaspoon fresh rosemary, chopped
- Salt and pepper to taste
- Lemon wedges for serving

Cooking Time: 25 minutes

Instructions:

1. Prepare the Marinade:
   - In a small bowl, combine the olive oil, lemon juice, minced garlic, chopped thyme, and rosemary. Season with salt and pepper to taste. Mix well to create a flavorful marinade.

2. Marinate the Sardines:

- Place the cleaned sardines in a shallow dish. Pour the prepared marinade over the sardines, ensuring they are well-coated. Let them marinate for at least 10 minutes, allowing the flavors to infuse.

3. Preheat the Grill:

- Preheat your grill to medium-high heat. Make sure the grates are clean and lightly oiled to prevent sticking.

4. Grill the Sardines:

- Carefully place the marinated sardines on the preheated grill. Grill for about 3-4 minutes per side, or until the fish is cooked through and has a nice char. The skin should be crispy, and the flesh should easily flake with a fork.

5. Serve with Lemon Wedges:

- Transfer the grilled sardines to a serving platter. Garnish with additional fresh herbs if desired and serve with lemon wedges on the side for a zesty touch.

Pro Tip:

- Cooking times may vary depending on the size of the sardines and the heat of your grill. Keep a close eye on them to ensure they are cooked to perfection.

Enjoy your seaside feast and savor the Mediterranean flavors of this quick and delightful grilled sardine recipe!

CHAPTER 56: SAFFRON-INFUSED SEAFOOD PAELLA

Ingredients:
- 2 cups Bomba rice
- 4 cups seafood or chicken broth
- 1 onion, finely chopped
- 4 cloves garlic, minced
- 1 red bell pepper, diced
- 1 yellow bell pepper, diced
- 1 cup frozen peas
- 1 tomato, diced
- 1/2 teaspoon saffron threads
- 1/2 teaspoon smoked paprika
- 1/2 teaspoon turmeric
- Salt and pepper to taste
- 1 pound mixed seafood (shrimp, squid, mussels, clams)
- 1/4 cup olive oil
- Lemon wedges for serving

Cooking Time: 30-35 minutes

Steps:

1. In a small bowl, combine the saffron threads with a tablespoon of warm water and let it steep.
2. Heat the olive oil in a large paella pan over medium heat. Add the onion and garlic, and sauté until softened.
3. Add the diced bell peppers and tomato to the pan, and cook until they begin to soften.
4. Stir in the rice, smoked paprika, turmeric, and saffron mixture. Cook for 1-2 minutes until the rice is well coated with the spices.
5. Pour in the seafood or chicken broth and bring the mixture to a boil. Reduce the heat to low and let it simmer for about 10 minutes, stirring occasionally.
6. Arrange the mixed seafood evenly over the rice mixture in the pan. Add the frozen peas on top.
7. Cover the pan with a lid or aluminum foil and let the paella cook for another 10-15 minutes, or until the rice is tender and the seafood is cooked through.
8. Once done, remove the lid and let the paella rest for a few minutes.
9. Serve hot with lemon wedges on the side.

Pro Prompt: Cooking times may vary based on your stove and the size of your paella pan. Keep an eye on the paella as it cooks to ensure the rice doesn't overcook or stick to the bottom of the pan. Enjoy the process and the aroma as your kitchen fills with the flavors of Spain!

CHAPTER 57: SMOKY PAPRIKA DEVILED EGGS

Ingredients:
- 6 hard-boiled eggs
- 3 tablespoons mayonnaise
- 1 teaspoon Dijon mustard
- 1 teaspoon smoked paprika
- Salt and pepper to taste
- Chopped chives for garnish

Cooking Time:Approximately 30 minutes

Steps:

1. Prepare Hard-Boiled Eggs:
  - Boil the eggs for 10-12 minutes until fully cooked.
  - Once done, cool, peel, and slice the eggs in half.

2. Remove Yolks:
  - Gently scoop out the egg yolks and place them in a bowl.

3. Create Filling:

- Mash the egg yolks with a fork.
- Add mayonnaise, Dijon mustard, smoked paprika, salt, and pepper.
- Mix until the filling is smooth and well combined.

4. Fill Egg Whites:

- Spoon or pipe the yolk mixture back into the egg whites.

5. Garnish:

- Sprinkle smoked paprika on top for an extra burst of flavor.
- Garnish with chopped chives for a fresh touch.

6. Serve:

- Arrange the deviled eggs on a plate and serve chilled.

Pro Tip:

- Experiment with the filling by adding a dash of hot sauce or finely chopped pickles for an extra kick.
- Watch the clock, as cooking times may vary based on your stove and egg size.

CHAPTER 58: CITRUS-INFUSED TIRAMISU CUPS

Ingredients:
- 1 cup strong brewed espresso, cooled
- 3 tablespoons orange liqueur
- 3 large egg yolks
- 3/4 cup granulated sugar
- 1 cup mascarpone cheese, softened
- 1 cup heavy whipping cream
- 1 teaspoon vanilla extract
- Zest of 1 orange
- Ladyfinger cookies
- Dark chocolate shavings for garnish

Steps:
1. In a shallow dish, combine the cooled espresso and orange liqueur. Set aside.
2. In a heatproof bowl, whisk together egg yolks and sugar. Place the bowl over a pot of simmering water, ensuring the bottom of the bowl doesn't touch the water. Whisk until the mixture becomes pale and slightly thickened.

3. Remove the bowl from heat and let it cool slightly. Incorporate the mascarpone cheese into the egg mixture until smooth.
4. In a separate bowl, whip the heavy cream with vanilla extract until stiff peaks form.
5. Gently fold the whipped cream into the mascarpone mixture until well combined. Add orange zest and mix gently.
6. Dip ladyfinger cookies into the espresso mixture, ensuring they are soaked but not soggy. Arrange a layer of dipped cookies at the bottom of serving cups.
7. Spoon a layer of the mascarpone mixture over the ladyfingers.
8. Repeat the process with another layer of dipped ladyfingers and mascarpone mixture until the cups are filled.
9. Cover and refrigerate for at least 4 hours or overnight to allow the flavors to meld.
10. Before serving, garnish with dark chocolate shavings.

Cooking Time:30 minutes (plus refrigeration time)

Pro Prompt: Each tiramisu cup is a symphony of flavors, but keep in mind that refrigeration time can vary. For an optimal taste experience, watch over your creation as time may differ based on your refrigerator temperature and personal preference for the creaminess of the dessert. Enjoy the anticipation of each delightful layer coming together!

CHAPTER 59: SAVORY SPINACH AND FETA STUFFED MUSHROOMS

Ingredients:
- 12 large white mushrooms, cleaned and stems removed
- 1 tablespoon olive oil
- 2 cloves garlic, minced
- 2 cups fresh spinach, chopped
- 1/2 cup feta cheese, crumbled
- Salt and pepper to taste
- 2 tablespoons breadcrumbs
- Fresh parsley, chopped, for garnish

Preparation Time: 10 minutes
Cooking Time: 20 minutes
Total Time:30 minutes

Instructions:

1. Preheat your oven to 375°F (190°C).

2. In a skillet, heat the olive oil over medium heat. Add the minced garlic and sauté for 1–2 minutes until fragrant.

3. Add the chopped spinach to the skillet and cook until wilted, about 3-4 minutes. Season with salt and pepper to taste.

4. Remove the skillet from heat and transfer the cooked spinach to a mixing bowl. Let it cool slightly.

5. Once the spinach has cooled, add the crumbled feta cheese to the bowl. Mix well to combine.

6. Stuff each mushroom cap with the spinach and feta mixture, pressing gently to fill the cavity.

7. Place the stuffed mushrooms on a baking sheet lined with parchment paper or lightly greased.

8. Sprinkle breadcrumbs over the stuffed mushrooms.

9. Bake in the preheated oven for 15-20 minutes, or until the mushrooms are tender and the filling is heated through.

10. Once done, remove the mushrooms from the oven and let them cool slightly.

11. Garnish with fresh chopped parsley before serving.

Pro Tip: Oven temperatures may vary, so keep an eye on the mushrooms towards the end of the cooking time to prevent them from overcooking. Adjust seasoning according to your taste preferences. Enjoy these savory stuffed mushrooms as a delightful appetizer or side dish for any occasion!

CHAPTER 60: ROASTED RED PEPPER AND TOMATO GAZPACHO

Ingredients:
- 6 ripe tomatoes, quartered
- 3 red bell peppers, halved and seeds removed
- 1 cucumber, peeled and chopped
- 1 small red onion, diced
- 2 cloves garlic, minced
- 4 cups tomato juice
- 1/4 cup red wine vinegar
- 1/3 cup extra-virgin olive oil
- Salt and pepper to taste
- Fresh basil leaves for garnish

Steps:
1. **Preheat Oven:** Preheat your oven to 400°F (200°C).

2. **Roast Vegetables:**Place the quartered tomatoes and halved red bell peppers on a baking sheet. Roast in the preheated oven for 25-30 minutes or until the skins are blistered and slightly charred.

3. **Cool and Peel:** Allow the roasted vegetables to cool. Once cooled, peel the skins off the tomatoes and remove the charred skin from the red peppers.

4. **Blend Ingredients:** In a blender, combine the roasted tomatoes, red peppers, cucumber, red onion, garlic, tomato juice, red wine vinegar, and olive oil. Blend until smooth.

5. **Season:** Season the gazpacho with salt and pepper to taste. Adjust the acidity with more red wine vinegar if needed.

6. **Chill:**Refrigerate the gazpacho for at least 2 hours to allow the flavors to meld.

7. **Serve:** Ladle the chilled gazpacho into bowls. Garnish with fresh basil leaves.

Total Time: Approximately 2.5 hours (Prep: 20 mins, Roasting: 30 mins, Chilling: 2 hours)

Pro Tip: The longer the gazpacho chills, the more intense the flavors become. For an extra burst of freshness, prepare it a day ahead.

Note to Readers: Cooking times may vary based on your equipment and preferences. Enjoy the process, and feel free to adjust the recipe to suit your taste. Watch for the magical transformation of flavors as the gazpacho chills – it's worth the wait!

CONCLUSION

In conclusion, the 30-Minute Andalusian Cookbook offers a diverse array of culinary delights that not only capture the essence of Spanish cuisine but also cater to the modern, time-conscious lifestyle. With over 100 recipes ranging from vibrant tapas to mouthwatering main courses and delectable desserts, this cookbook is a treasure trove of quick and flavorful dishes.

The recipes presented in the cookbook showcase the beauty of Andalusian flavors, with a particular emphasis on efficiency without compromising on taste. Whether you're a seasoned chef or a cooking enthusiast, the step-by-step instructions, varied ingredients, and time-efficient techniques ensure a delightful cooking experience.

Each chapter invites you to embark on a culinary journey, exploring the rich tapestry of Andalusian cuisine. From the sizzling starters to the tempting tarts, every recipe is crafted to be prepared in around 30 minutes, making it accessible for busy individuals who seek a taste of the Mediterranean without spending hours in the kitchen.

As you delve into the cookbook, experiment with the vibrant ingredients, savor the aromatic spices, and relish the simplicity of creating impressive dishes in a short amount of time. The 30-Minute Andalusian Cookbook is not just a collection of recipes; it's an invitation to embrace the joy of cooking, savoring the rich flavors of Spain, and making every meal a celebration of culinary artistry.